THE FUTURE OF
Artificial Intelligence
(AI) IN MUSIC
PRODUCTION

Dedication

Dare to push the boundaries of what is possible, dreamers, creators, innovators.

To the musicians finding their voice in every note and rhythm, to the technologists who build the tools that bring those sounds to life, and to those who believe the future of music is a harmonious blend of human emotion and AI.

To my family, friends, and mentors, who showed relentless support and encouragement throughout the journey that made this possible.

This book is for you.

Contents

Introduction

The Convergence of Music and Technology

Music has been integrated into human culture for thousands of years now. It involves the universal language between the borders which connects people on a relatively profound aspect. History has been a witness to the changes in the procedure created for numbering music ever since the invention of instruments to recording studios, which has been integrated due to technological development. CFI, we now stand at the threshold of a new age in music production, driven by the transformative power of AI.

Imagine AI systems that write breathtaking melodies, fine-tune audio recordings to perfection—now even collaborating with other musicians while on air. But what once may have seemed to be only possible far off in the future happening right before our very ears. This is the very relationship that music keeps with technology, relentlessly evolving into new dimensions with AI innovation, changing the very fabrics of both creation and experiences with sounds that people share today.

AI and the Future of Music Production

Recently, AI has gone so far, deriving benefits in multiple other fields that it added to the music industry as well. AI algorithms and machine learning models now understand the fine art of musical composition and complex audio data together with many other assistant roles of musicians and producers that people could never dream about. It ranges from composing pieces to the modification of sound quality and personalized recommendations for playlists, changing every single process in music production.

Harmonizing Innovation: The Future of AI in Music Production — this book is your gateway to an exuberant land where creativity and artificial intelligence meet. Over the next 30 pages, we embark on a fascinating journey about the impact of AI on the music business. We dive deep into the super-interesting sphere of AI-driven music composition, in which AI is bringing revolution to sound engineering. So, look into the potential of collaboration between humans and AI in the music industry.

However, this is not only a technical exploration; it is equally a glimpse into the artistry of what is to come. We will unveil how music recommendations will be tailored to one's unique taste by AI and make open new worlds of music to you. How AI-Driven Music Marketing is connecting artists with their audiences in ways never before; huge data sets are mined by algorithms for insights that were unimaginable.

But as we usher in this new dawn, we find ourselves facing a number of attendant ethical questions. How do we deal with copyright in the production of music in the AI world? What are the ethics of AI working with artists? Those are the kind of questions we'll be dealing with as we strike a balance between creativity and automation.

Your Journey to the Future of Music

As we embark on this journey regarding the future of AI in music making, it is important to keep an open mind. The boundaries of possibilities tend to grow ceaselessly, and the music industry is at the forefront of this technological renaissance.

Whether you are a musician in search of new horizons, a music producer who wants to use the power of AI, or simply an amateur eager to understand the changing soundscape, this book will bring enlightenment, inspiration, and set your imagination on fire. We take a journey into those potentials of AI that shape the melodies of tomorrow, respecting artistry as it defines music to be a unique form of human expression.

So, buckle up, because today we're off into the consonant world of AI-invigorated music production—an Eden where the future of music awaits you, offering your part to play within this symphony of innovation.

Chapter 1: AI-Powered Music Composition

From Mozart to Machines: The Evolution of Music Composition

The art of melody, harmony, and rhythm creation, music composition has long been accorded ranking among the deepest forms of human creativity. The process of music making, from classic works by Mozart and Beethoven to the experiments of current musicians, has always been inhuman hands. It has been inspired, emotional, and worked out by the intuitive genius of composers.

But it is this journey through the digital age that we find ourselves at a remarkable crossroads where human creativity meets AI. It is a celebration of this crossroad that this chapter enters: an exploration of just how AI, this product of human minds, is reinventing the virtual wheel when it comes to music composition.

The Evolution of Music Composition

Music composition, as we understand it, is an act that has a rich history spanning thousands of years. The progress in the musical style, technique, and form has been contributed to by one era towards another. Composers reflect on their environment and feelings or cultural forces to bequeath generations with creations that stand the test of time.

The Classical period brought works by composers such as Mozart, Haydn, and Beethoven, who worked in such rigid forms as sonatas and symphonies. Romantic composers, on the other hand, such as Chopin and Wagner, stressed passionate expression and expanded the size of the instruments in their orchestra.

In the 20th century, there were unprecedented experiments in music composition with the avant-garde technique, electronic sounds, and genocide of genres. Some of the most creative composers in the period were born Igor Stravinsky and John Cage, questioning conventional thoughts in music.

Across the sweep of this history, there was one thing that never changed: the human creative impulse at the core of composition. The composer translated thoughts and feelings, turning stories into musical notes and harmonies that became works able to touch people in the highest possible way.

AI Is Changing Music Composition

We are on the verge of a new era in music composition history, defined by the combination of AI. Being powered by advanced algorithms and machine learning, AI takes a great leap forward into what is possible with music creation.

In this chapter, we look into how AI is revolutionizing the very process of music composition. We will explore to what extent AI can dig deeply into broad musical data sets, thus creating brand new musical pieces and even emulating the very best composers themselves. We will see AI-based tools that help musicians find new wellsprings of inspiration and tread into worlds of creativity they wouldn't even have thought to go into.

However, this only implies augmentation of creativity and not replacement of the human composer. AI is one of the collaborators, a fellow in the creation process. It can offer a composer new tools, provide help in proposing new musical ideas, and speed up the composition process.

As we delve deeper into the world of AI-assisted composition, we will see some truly striking examples of music written with AI, learn about the journeys of composers who came to adopt the technology, and, of course, learn what the future might hold. Humans and machines unite in influence—and thus form the music of tomorrow—making it one of the great symphonies of innovation and art.

Join us in the journey of how AI has impacted music composition. It is the foray that spans centuries of tradition into the limitless creative world of AI: from Mozart to machines—the evolution of music composition.

The history of music composition is essentially a tapestry woven with the threads of creativity, innovation, and human expression. It is a journey from the grand symphonies of Mozart to the intricate electronic landscapes that contemporary artists draw. Music has always functioned as an art that is massively connected with human experience vis-à-vis basic emotions, stories, and cultural movements that melodies and harmonies have carried throughout the eras.

The Classical period, between the mid-18th to early 19th century, was a crucial period in musical composition. Wolfgang Amadeus Mozart, Ludwig van Beethoven, and Joseph Haydn were among the central figures of this period.

Mozart The Child Prodigy: Wolfgang Amadeus Mozart, as we know, was a child prodigy. His works are marked by an exquisite formal perfection along with emotional depth, leaving an imprint on the profoundly great music of the classics. Works like "Eine Kleine Nachtmusik" and "Symphony No. 40" are a prime example of Mozart's craft at creating unforgettable melodies within clear forms.

Beethoven: Pushing the Limits Ludwig van Beethoven is often considered to be a link between the Classical era and the Romantic era. His penchant for pushing the boundaries of the possible in composing music can perhaps be best represented by his Ninth Symphony, the final movement of which is a choral rendition of An die Freude, a love song to joy. His works were highly emotional and manifested new explorations of harmony.

Haydn: Father of the Symphony Joseph Haydn is often referred to as the "Father of the Symphony" as an instrumental composer. He was very inventive in his use of sound devices. His symphonies often show wit and invention, attempting to perfect styles that many of the composers following him would be prone to follow.

The 19th century brought with it attitudes toward emotional expression and individualism, moving music into the Romantic era and stressing such attitudes. Composers such as Frédéric Chopin, Pyotr Ilyich Tchaikovsky, and Richard Wagner delved deeply into human emotionality in their compositions.

Chopin: The Poet of the Piano Since the time of Frédéric Chopin, the piano has always been viewed as a lyrical instrument. His music abounds in lyrical beauty and emotional depth. Works like the Nocturnes and Ballades are examples of how he was able to bring out the most delicate and sensitive emotions through his music.

Wagner: Epic Grandeur Richard Wagner's operas, including "Tristan und Isolde" and "The Ring Cycle," were perhaps the most innovative that the musical drama had ever seen. It was through the same leitmotifs, in conjunction with its epic scale, which opera was turned into a discursive narrative art.

Experimentalism and Innovation: The 20th Century

Music composition took a big turn during the 20th century. Experimentation became the name of the game, with dissonance, atonality, and electronic sounds now having a place in compositions.

Stravinsky: Rhythm and Ritual The choral ballet of Igor Stravinsky, "The Rite of Spring," was an absolute outrage of complex rhythm and an expansion on the simple definition of music. It truly was a groundbreaking modern composer.

Cage: Music as a Concept John Cage really challenged the concept of performing music by creating pieces such as "4'33," in which no sound ever comes from the oratorio, and the guests are instead required to listen to the sounds of nature.

The 21st Century: AI and Fresh New Horizons

As we stand at the threshold of the 21st century, a new era is being unveiled: that of music composition, set off by the infusion of AI into the scenario. Powerful algorithms and machine learning in AI are stretching the envelope of what actually can be done with music production. In this brave new world, creativity and innovation know no bounds; what ensues is a harmonious blend of tradition and technology.

Looking at the chapters which follow, we shall see in what way AI is changing the very landscape of the flowchart of musical composition. We will see how AI algorithms come up with their pieces in the way that Mozart did, and also how AI will direct new creative routes for musicians. More importantly, though, we shall celebrate the indomitable spirit of human creativity that has driven music-making from Mozart's time up to this age of machines.

The history of music composition shows the human imagination and innovation at its best. A history of how the music permutated, mutated, and re-envisioned itself through centuries, and this journey does not seem to stop any bit with the infusion of AI. Now, with a digital pulse, let us remember that the heart beats at the center of music composition.

How AI Is Changing Music Composition

In the 21st century, we now stand at the crossroads of two great forces: the time-honored creativity of human composers and the computational power of AI. The result is the birth of a new era called music composition—an era defined by innovation, collaboration, and the possible infinity of AI-induced creativity.

AI as Co-Creator

AI does not replace human creators of music but rather becomes its collaborator. A purely digital partner that is able to assist, inspire, and broaden the horizons of music creation; here is how it's changing that sphere of composition forever:

AI-Generated Music: Algorithms have the ability to write original music pieces. AI systems scrutinize gargantuan datasets of existing compositions, identify patterns, and create new melodies, harmonies, and rhythms. Works thus produced can range from Classical to very contemporary idioms, demonstrating AI's creative adaptability.

2. Style Imitation: AI can mimic the styles of the great composers. Do you want something in the style of Mozart, Bach, or Beethoven? AI can analyze their works and generate compositions that follow their unique stylistic signatures.

3. Instant Inspiration: Composers suffer from creative blocks. AI can provide instant inspiration by suggesting melodies, chord progressions,

or instrumentation ideas according to the preferences of the composer or any particular topic.

4. Algorithmic Compositions: Composers can exploit AI algorithms toward the creation of complex and exploratory compositions. AI would develop complex musical structures surpassing the scope of what is done in Classical pieces, leading to completely new avant-garde and experimental pieces.

5. Real-Time Collaboration: Just take a moment to consider how exciting it would be to work on a real-time collaboration project with an AI system. Musicians play or sing, and AIs reply with harmonies, agree with the chords, or suggest lyrics. This would really open new horizons for improvisation on the fly, which is part of the excitement of live music.

6. Endless Variations: AI can produce endless varieties of a musical theme, making it an invaluable tool for film scoring, video game soundtracks, and background music, where composers would require a vast collection of options to suit varying scenes or moods.

Enhancing the Creative Process

AI does not really compose; it augments the entire creative process:

1. Arrangement and Orchestration: Take a simple tune and turn it into some full orchestral arrangement. Composers could try several instrumentations and arrangements, dramatically quickening the compositional process toward a greater diversity of ensembles.

2. Melody Harmonization: The user inputs a melody, and the AI harmonizes it in different styles. It greatly aids musicians in exploring further opportunities harmonically for their compositions.

3. Lyric Generation: The AI can support the lyricist by suggesting rhymes, themes, or even writing the entire lyrics on a given topic or emotion available in the input.

4. Sound Design: AI-assisted sound design tools create unique artificial soundscapes and effects that bring composition to life with depth and character. Now, musicians can play with AI-generated sounds to create sounds that are so different in texture.

Impacts on Music Education

AI is also taking over forms of music education:

1. AI Tutors: The AI tutor can provide personally crafted courses to teach musicians. For example, they can teach a student how to play musical instruments, music theories, or voice culture.

2. Music Analysis: AI can check and analyze the way a student plays to provide feedback on the balancing of techniques, controlling timing, or expression, which increases the possibility of quick and better learning.

Problems and Ethical Issues

AI holds new opportunities for music composition but poses some serious questions:

1. Copyright and Ownership: Who owns AI-generated music, the composer, AI developers, or both? The legal and ethical considerations of AI-generated music are not straightforward.

2. Authenticity: This has been one of the main arguments so far—to say that AI-composed music cannot really give the genuine articulation and depth of emotion that human-created compositions offer. Balancing human and AI creativity is an ongoing challenge.

3. Artistic Value: What is the artistic value to AI-generated music? Is it an artistic tool for inspiration, or is it a serious form of musical expression?

The Future of AI in Music Composition

As AI grows and develops further, music composition with AI will rise in potential and scope. There will be ways to combine creativity and technology that musicians, composers, and AI developers will seek and find. It will be a collaboration between humans in art with AI at peak innovation—a symphonic interplay fostering endless possibilities.

In these next chapters, the different aspects of comprehensive AI in music composition are delved into with practical examples, successful collaborations, and ongoing debates about AI use in this creative domain. Well, then, let's watch music meet machines right before our eyes in a way that will change the landscape, and human imagination dance with AI.

This chapter presents a clear, wide view of how AI is taking shape in music production as a collaborator and enabler of the creative process. The last section identifies current and future challenges and describes safeguards needed to ensure the ethical making of music under AI dominance, setting the scene for several chapters about specific AI applications in music.

Case Studies: AI Composers in Action

Where technology and creativity meet lies the domain of AI composers, and this has finally shaped melodies, harmonies, and compositions that hold audiences globally. Let's go through some interesting case studies which prove the importance of AI in music composition.

1. Amper Music: Composition at Fingertips with AI

Background: Amper Music is an AI music composition platform that allows musicians, content creators, and producers to compose originally engineered music with the help of AI. A user is entitled to put in their creative preferences regarding style, mood, instrumentation, and so on; then, with its AI, Amper generates fully orchestrated compositions that fit the specifications.

Impact: Amper Music has democratized music composition by providing top-notch, custom-made music for any projects by its creators with the most minimal musical background. Industry applications have been realized within movies and advertisement all the way through video games, providing rapid music production with creative flexibility.

Notable Projects:

• **Game of Thrones:** An advertisement promo for the hit TV series "Game of Thrones" was scored with Amper Music, really showing the potential of creating epic and cinematic music.

• **Video Games:** Indie game developers have used Amper AI in a number of ways to create unique soundtracks for their games, really enhancing the gaming experience all around.

2. Aiva: AI-Generated Classical Compositions

Background: Aiva is an AI music creation platform oriented towards producing Classical music pieces. Deep learning algorithms are combined with rich databases of Classical scores to create original pieces in the style of Classical masters.

Impact: Aiva has won international acclaim by composing Classical music which cannot be distinguished from that composed by a human mind. Aiva thus opens a window for new Classical composition and brings some revival to the traditional Classical path with a modern twist.

Notable Projects:

• Concert Performances: Aiva's compositions were played in concert halls by orchestras, showing the world that AIs can create music that moves audiences and musicians alike.

• Independent Film Soundtracks: Aiva's Classical pieces have been placed as soundtracks in independent films and have created modern cinematic experiences with unique and Classical feels.

3. OpenAI's MuseNet: Extending Musical Frontiers

Background: OpenAI's MuseNet is a deep learning model that generates music in quite diverse styles and genres, from Classical and jazz to pop and rock. It helps users look into the immense possibilities of music.

Impact: MuseNet has really been able to push the boundaries with respect to AI-generated music by powering music creation in wide diversities of style and genre. It empowers musicians and composers to try out various ideas in music and stretch creative horizons and test boundaries.

Some Exciting Projects:

• Genre Exploration: In this case, musicians and composers used MuseNet to get deeper into genres with which they wouldn't have been familiar otherwise and created unique, innovative pieces.

• Collaborative Experimentation: MuseNet has always been a collaborative tool, but now it enables the opportunity for collaboration among musicians of very different backgrounds to come together and create music, smashing genres and styles in unexpected ways.

These case studies demonstrate how AI composers are involved in today's music composition landscape. They show the versatility and impact AI has on producing music that is at once creative and technically impressive. As we move into the future with AI in music composition, these examples set a basis for how human creativity and artificial intelligence can collaborate.

These case studies epitomize how AI composers can be seen in action, showing the way ahead toward influencing vast industries from entertainment to Classical music. They showcase the impact and flexibility of AI in the arena of music composition.

Chapter 2: AI in Sound Engineering

Unlocking the Sonic Frontier with AI

Sound engineering, the art of capturing, processing, and enhancing audio, has long been the backbone of the music and entertainment industry. Whether it's the crystal-clear vocals of a pop ballad, the thunderous explosions in a blockbuster movie, or the immersive ambiance of a video game, sound engineers shape the auditory experiences that define our multimedia world.

In this chapter, we dive into the fascinating world where technology meets audio craftsmanship. We explore the transformative role of AI in sound engineering—a space where algorithms analyze, process, and enhance audio with remarkable precision and speed.

The Sound Engineer's Toolkit

Sound engineers are known for their meticulous attention to detail, their finely tuned ears, and their ability to craft sonic experiences that resonate with audiences. Traditionally, they have relied on a vast array of tools and techniques, from equalizers and compressors to reverbs and spatialization.

AI is ushering in a new era, where these tools are not just instruments but intelligent collaborators. AI algorithms can identify imperfections in audio recordings, correct pitch and timing issues, and even emulate the acoustics of legendary recording studios. They work tirelessly to ensure that every note, every sound effect, and every voice is precisely where it should be, creating audio that is pristine and immersive.

The AI Advantage in Sound Engineering

AI's impact on sound engineering is profound:

1. **Noise Reduction and Restoration:** AI algorithms can identify and eliminate unwanted noise in audio recordings, restoring clarity and fidelity. This is invaluable in situations where pristine audio is critical, such as in music production, film post-production, and podcasting.

2. **Audio Enhancement:** AI can automatically enhance audio by adjusting levels, equalizing frequencies, and optimizing spatialization. It ensures that audio recordings sound at their best without the need for extensive manual adjustments.

3. **Pitch Correction:** AI-driven pitch correction tools are widely used in the music industry to fine-tune vocal performances and instrument recordings. They can correct subtle pitch variations or create creative pitch effects.

4. **Voice Separation:** AI can isolate individual voices or instruments in a mixed audio track, allowing for precise control during remixing or post-production work.

5. **Sound Synthesis:** AI models can synthesize realistic sounds and instruments, expanding the possibilities for composers and sound designers. This opens up new avenues for creating original audio content.

AI in Live Sound: In live sound engineering, AI can analyze and adapt audio in real-time, adjusting levels, EQ, and effects to ensure optimal sound quality for concertgoers. It's like having an audio engineer on standby, continuously optimizing the sonic experience.

AI-Enhanced Audio Effects: AI-powered audio effects, such as reverbs and spatialization algorithms, can create immersive soundscapes that enhance the impact of music, movies, and games.

In this chapter, we'll delve deeper into each of these areas, exploring real world examples and applications of AI in sound engineering. We'll witness how AI is reshaping the way audio is produced, ensuring that every sonic nuance is polished to perfection. As we journey through the AI-enhanced world of sound engineering, we'll discover a symphony of possibilities and creativity, where human expertise and AI innovation harmoniously blend.

Join us as we unravel the AI-driven transformation of sound engineering—a journey that promises to redefine audio quality, precision, and artistry.

This introduction to Chapter 2 sets the stage for exploring the significant role of AI in sound engineering. It highlights how AI is revolutionizing audio processing, enhancement, and optimization, ultimately contributing to the creation of immersive auditory experiences in various multimedia domains.

The Art and Science of Sound Engineering

Sound engineering is a multifaceted discipline that lies at the intersection of art and science. It's a craft that encompasses both technical expertise and creative intuition, where the manipulation of sound waves transforms raw audio into mesmerizing auditory experiences that captivate our senses. In this section, we'll explore the artistry and scientific precision that define sound engineering.

The Craftsmanship of Sound

Sound engineers are the unsung heroes behind the scenes of music production, film post-production, live concerts, and countless other audio-centric endeavors. They wield a range of tools and techniques to shape sound, each choice made with precision and purpose.

1. **Capturing the Moment:** Sound engineers are responsible for capturing sound at its source, whether it's a live concert performance, a dialogue scene in a film, or a recording session in a studio. This process involves selecting the right microphones, positioning them strategically, and adjusting settings to capture the nuances of sound.

2. **The Art of Mixing:** Mixing is where science meets art. Sound engineers adjust the levels, equalization, panning, and effects to create a balanced and cohesive sonic experience. They sculpt soundscapes that allow each element—vocals, instruments, and effects—to shine while ensuring they blend harmoniously.

3. **Mastering Mastery:** The final step in the audio production process is mastering, where engineers apply the finishing touches. This involves optimizing the overall sound quality, ensuring consistency across tracks, and preparing audio for distribution.

The Science Behind Sound

While sound engineering is undoubtedly an art form, it's equally grounded in scientific principles. Understanding the physics of sound waves, acoustics, and audio technology is essential for achieving professional results.

1. **Sound Waves:** Sound engineers need to grasp the fundamental properties of sound waves—frequency, amplitude, wavelength, and

phase. This knowledge informs decisions about audio processing, equalization, and effects.

2. **Acoustic Environments:** An understanding of acoustics is crucial for optimizing sound quality in various spaces. Sound engineers consider how sound waves interact with the environment, such as room reflections, to create the desired sonic atmosphere.

3. **Audio Technology:** Sound engineers work with a plethora of audio equipment, from analog consoles to digital audio workstations (DAWs) and software plugins. Staying up to date with technological advancements is a constant pursuit.

4. **Psychoacoustics:** Sound engineers must also be aware of psychoacoustic principles, which relate to how the human brain perceives and interprets sound. This knowledge guides decisions about audio placement, effects, and spatialization to create immersive listening experiences.

The Harmonious Fusion

What sets apart exceptional sound engineers is their ability to seamlessly merge the technical and artistic aspects of their craft. They leverage their scientific understanding of sound to make creative choices that elevate audio to new heights.

1. **Creative Effects:** Sound engineers use a palette of effects—reverb, delay, modulation, and more—to craft unique sonic textures. These effects are not just technical tools; they are artistic brushstrokes that shape the auditory canvas.

2. **Emotion and Storytelling:** Sound engineers are storytellers. They use music, sound effects, and audio cues to evoke emotions, enhance narratives, and immerse audiences in the world of film, games, and other media.

3. **Live Sound Engineering:** In live concert settings, sound engineers are akin to conductors, ensuring that every note and instrument is heard with clarity and precision. Their technical prowess enables musicians to shine on stage.

4. **Collaboration and Communication:** Effective communication with artists, directors, and producers is a hallmark of skilled sound engineers. They understand the vision and translate it into sound.

The Future of Sound Engineering: AI as a Partner

As we delve deeper into this book, we'll explore the transformative role of AI in sound engineering. AI is not replacing the artistry of sound engineering; it's enhancing it. AI algorithms can analyze audio, identify imperfections, suggest creative enhancements, and even automate repetitive tasks, freeing sound engineers to focus on the creative nuances.

Join us as we navigate the intricacies of sound engineering, where the fusion of art and science yields auditory masterpieces that leave a lasting impact. In the chapters to come, we'll explore how AI is becoming an indispensable partner in this captivating world, unlocking new dimensions of audio artistry and precision.

This section provides an in-depth look into the artistry and scientific foundations of sound engineering. It sets the stage for the integration of AI in sound engineering, highlighting how AI complements the creativity and technical expertise of sound engineers.

Enhanced Soundscapes: AI-Generated Effects and Enhancements

Soundscapes are auditory landscapes that transport us to different worlds, evoke emotions, and immerse us in the stories told through music, film, and gaming. In the field of sound engineering, creating rich and immersive soundscapes is a fundamental goal. Now, with the integration of AI, sound engineers are equipped with powerful tools to elevate soundscapes to unprecedented levels of depth and creativity.

The Power of Immersion

Immersive soundscapes are the backbone of cinematic experiences, video games, virtual reality, and music production. They transport audiences into the heart of a story, setting the stage for emotional connection and engagement. AI is revolutionizing the way sound engineers craft these immersive environments.

1. **3D Audio and Spatialization:** AI algorithms can analyze audio and apply spatialization effects that mimic real world sound propagation. This means that sounds can move dynamically around the listener, creating a sense of space and dimension. Whether it's the rustling leaves in a forest or the echoes in a vast cave, AI-enhanced spatialization brings environments to life.

2. **Environmental Effects:** AI can generate realistic environmental effects, such as rain, wind, or thunder, that seamlessly blend with audio recordings. These effects add depth and authenticity to soundscapes, making them more convincing and engaging.

3. **Ambisonics:** Ambisonics is a technique that captures audio from all directions, providing a 360-degree soundscape. AI can process Ambisonics recordings to create immersive audio experiences that envelop listeners.

The Art of Audio Effects

Sound engineers have long relied on audio effects to shape soundscapes, from reverb and delay to modulation and compression. AI takes these effects to the next level by making them smarter and more adaptive.

1. **AI-Powered Reverb:** AI algorithms can analyze the acoustic properties of virtual spaces and apply reverb effects that are indistinguishable from real world acoustics. This allows sound engineers to tailor reverb precisely to the desired atmosphere, whether it's a cathedral's grandeur or a cozy living room's intimacy.

2. **Dynamic Mixing:** AI-powered dynamic mixing adjusts audio levels, equalization, and effects in real-time, optimizing sound quality for the listener's environment. This is particularly valuable for live events and interactive media where audio conditions vary.

3. **Voice Separation:** AI can separate individual voices and instruments in a mixed audio track, giving sound engineers precise control over each element. This capability is a game-changer for remixing, post-production, and adaptive audio experiences.

The Collaborative Symphony

AI doesn't replace the artistry of sound engineers; it amplifies it. Sound engineers collaborate with AI systems to achieve new heights of creativity and precision.

1. **Creative Suggestions:** AI can suggest creative effects and enhancements based on the desired mood or genre, helping sound engineers explore new sonic territories.

2. **Time Efficiency:** AI automates repetitive tasks, allowing sound engineers to focus on the creative nuances of sound design and mixing. This efficiency accelerates the production process.

3. **Adaptive Sound:** In interactive media like video games and virtual reality, AI adapts audio in real-time based on user actions and environment changes, ensuring a consistent and immersive experience.

The Future of Soundscapes

As we look to the future, AI is poised to redefine the possibilities of soundscapes. Innovations such as AI-generated music and dynamic audio rendering will push the boundaries of creativity and interactivity. Sound engineers and AI are becoming inseparable partners, co-creators of sonic experiences that leave lasting impressions on audiences.

Join us as we explore the dynamic world of AI-generated effects and enhancements in sound engineering. In the chapters ahead, we'll delve into real world applications, success stories, and the limitless potential of AI in crafting soundscapes that captivate, thrill, and inspire.

This section provides an in-depth look into how AI is enhancing soundscapes through the generation of effects and enhancements. It highlights the transformative role of AI in creating immersive auditory experiences and the collaborative partnership between AI and sound engineers.

Harmonizing with Machines: The Future of Musical Collaboration

Music, at its core, is a collaborative art form—a timeless dialogue between composers, musicians, and audiences. The creative process often involves musicians interpreting a composer's vision and adding their unique artistic flair. But what if this ensemble included a new member: AI? In this chapter, we embark on a journey into the evolving landscape of musical collaboration, where human ingenuity harmonizes with machine intelligence.

The Age-Old Tradition of Collaboration

Throughout history, music collaboration has taken myriad forms. Composers have worked closely with performers to bring their compositions to life. Jazz improvisation thrives on spontaneous collaboration among musicians. And in modern music production, collaboration extends to producers, engineers, and even songwriters.

In this grand tradition of musical cooperation, AI emerges as a powerful collaborator. It's not a replacement for human musicians or composers but an additional creative voice—a partner that offers fresh insights, novel ideas, and the ability to push musical boundaries.

AI as a Composer's Muse

AI has the remarkable capacity to inspire and guide composers in exciting new directions:

1. **Creative Sparks:** AI algorithms can generate melodies, chord progressions, and harmonies that spark the imagination of composers. They provide a wealth of ideas to explore, helping composers break through creative blocks.

2. **Style Exploration:** AI can mimic the styles of renowned composers, from Bach to The Beatles. Composers can experiment with different musical eras and genres, expanding their artistic palette.

3. **Arrangement Assistance:** Composers often grapple with arranging their compositions for different instruments and ensembles. AI can offer suggestions and assist in crafting intricate arrangements.

4. **Lyric Generation:** For songwriters, AI can suggest lyrics, themes, and even generate complete verses and choruses. It's a wellspring of inspiration for crafting compelling narratives.

5. **Endless Variations:** AI can generate variations of a musical theme, allowing composers to explore different musical directions and experiment with motifs and motifs.

AI in Ensemble Play

In the art of live music performance, AI is becoming a capable ensemble player:

1. **Virtual Collaborators:** Musicians can perform alongside AI systems that respond in real-time, generating accompaniments, harmonies, and even improvisations. It's a dynamic form of musical interaction.

2. **Musical Assistants:** AI can act as musical assistants during rehearsals, helping musicians stay in tune, maintain tempo, and navigate complex compositions.

3. **Interactive Performances:** In live concerts, AI can analyze audience reactions and adapt the performance in real-time, creating interactive and engaging musical experiences.

AI and the Music Industry

The music industry, too, is embracing AI as a collaborator:

1. **AI-Generated Music:** AI is producing original compositions that are used in film scores, advertisements, and even standalone music albums.

2. **Recommendation Systems:** Streaming platforms leverage AI to recommend music tailored to individual tastes, connecting listeners with new artists and genres.

3. **Music Production Tools:** AI-powered software and plugins aid music producers in sound design, mixing, and mastering, streamlining the production process.

A Journey of Exploration

Join us in this exploration of AI and music collaboration, where we uncover the stories of composers who have embraced AI as a muse and musicians who have shared the stage with intelligent algorithms. We'll delve into the creative synergies between humans and machines, the evolving landscape of AI-generated music, and the opportunities that arise when we harmonize with the digital minds of the future.

As we navigate the uncharted waters of AI-infused musical collaboration, we'll discover that the music of tomorrow is a symphony of human creativity and machine ingenuity—a harmonious blend of the past, present, and future.

Chapter 3- AI and Music Collaboration

Music is a universal language that transcends boundaries and speaks to the depths of the human soul. It has been shaped by generations of composers, performers, and listeners, each contributing their unique voice to this eternal conversation. In the modern era, this dialogue has taken a fascinating turn as AI joins the ranks of collaborators, offering new perspectives, creative insights, and the potential to redefine the musical landscape.

A Symphony of Collaboration

Musical collaboration is a time-honored tradition. Composers collaborate with performers to bring their compositions to life, bands harmonize to create iconic melodies, and producers sculpt soundscapes in the studio. AI steps onto this grand stage as a versatile partner, enriching the creative process.

1. **AI as the Muse:** AI algorithms can inspire composers with melodies, chord progressions, and harmonies. They offer a wellspring of ideas, breaking through creative blocks and expanding the boundaries of musical imagination.

2. **Stylistic Exploration:** AI can mimic the styles of legendary composers, from Classical maestros to modern hitmakers. Composers can journey through different musical eras and genres, experimenting with new sonic textures.

3. **Arrangement Assistance:** Crafting arrangements for various instruments and ensembles can be a complex task. AI can provide suggestions and assist in orchestrating intricate compositions.

4. **Lyric Generation:** For songwriters, AI is a lyrical companion, suggesting themes, rhymes, and even generating entire verses and choruses. It's a wellspring of inspiration for crafting compelling narratives.

5. **Endless Variations:** AI generates variations of musical themes, allowing composers to explore different directions and experiment with motifs and motifs.

AI as an Ensemble Player

Live music performance takes on a new dimension with AI as an ensemble player:

1. **Virtual Collaborators:** Musicians can perform alongside AI systems that respond in real-time, generating accompaniments, harmonies, and even improvisations. It's a dynamic form of musical interaction that blurs the line between human and machine.

2. **Musical Assistants:** AI acts as a helpful assistant during rehearsals, aiding musicians in staying in tune, maintaining tempo, and navigating complex compositions.

3. **Interactive Performances:** In live concerts, AI analyzes audience reactions and adapts the performance on the fly, creating interactive and engaging musical experiences that respond to the energy of the crowd.

AI and the Music Industry

The music industry itself has embraced AI as a collaborator and innovator:

1. **AI-Generated Music:** AI is composing original pieces used in film scores, advertisements, and standalone music albums. It's a testament to the versatility of AI in producing music across genres and styles.

2. **Recommendation Systems:** Streaming platforms employ AI to recommend music tailored to individual tastes, connecting listeners with new artists and genres. These recommendations have reshaped how we discover and enjoy music.

3. **Music Production Tools:** AI-powered software and plugins have become indispensable tools for music producers. They assist in sound design, mixing, and mastering, streamlining the production process and opening new creative possibilities.

The Collaborative Revolution

The synergy between humans and AI in music collaboration represents a transformative shift in the creative process. It's not about machines replacing musicians but amplifying their creativity. The dialogue between human composers, performers, and AI algorithms results in compositions that push the boundaries of musical innovation.

As we embark on this exploration of AI and music collaboration, we'll uncover the stories of composers who have embraced AI as a muse and musicians who have shared the stage with intelligent algorithms. Together, we'll navigate the uncharted waters of this collaborative revolution, where the music of tomorrow is a symphony of human creativity and machine ingenuity—a harmonious blend of the past, present, and future.

This section provides an in-depth look into the evolving landscape of AI and music collaboration, emphasizing the symbiotic relationship between human creativity and AI intelligence in the world of music. It showcases how AI serves as an inspiring partner for composers, performers, and the music industry, contributing to innovative and boundary-pushing musical expressions.

Exploring the Boundaries: Human-AI Collaborations in Music

Music has always been a reflection of human creativity, a canvas where artists paint their emotions, stories, and dreams with melodies and harmonies. The evolution of music, however, is not bound by tradition alone. It's a dynamic journey where technology continually reshapes the boundaries of what is possible. In the field of music, AI is the new frontier—a creative partner that challenges conventions, expands horizons, and takes us on a harmonious exploration of the unknown.

The Convergence of Minds

Human-AI collaborations in music represent a convergence of two creative forces. It's a journey where composers, performers, and producers invite AI algorithms to join the ensemble, creating harmonies that resonate with both the heart and the machine.

1. **Compositional Creativity:** AI algorithms generate musical ideas that act as a muse for composers. They offer melodies, harmonies, and rhythms that inspire compositions and push artistic boundaries.

2. **Performance Innovation:** Musicians share the stage with AI systems, engaging in dynamic improvisations and co-creating music in real-time. It's a fusion of human expression and algorithmic spontaneity.

3. **Production Efficiency:** Music producers harness AI-powered tools that streamline sound design, mixing, and mastering. This efficiency liberates creative energy for experimentation and innovation.

4. **Interactive Experiences:** AI transforms live performances into interactive experiences, where music adapts to audience reactions, creating a unique connection between artist and listener.

AI as an Inspirational Muse

For composers, AI is a wellspring of inspiration:

1. **Melodic Sparks:** AI algorithms generate melodies and harmonies, offering fresh ideas that composers can build upon. They provide a treasure trove of musical possibilities.

2. **Stylistic Exploration:** AI can mimic the styles of legendary composers, enabling composers to experiment with different musical eras and genres, from Baroque to electronic dance music.

3. **Arrangement Assistance:** Crafting arrangements for various instruments and ensembles becomes more accessible with AI suggestions, allowing composers to explore intricate compositions.

4. **Lyric Insights:** For songwriters, AI can suggest lyrics, themes, and rhymes, offering a pool of creative concepts to draw from.

5. **Endless Variations:** AI generates variations of musical themes, opening doors to explore different directions and experiment with motifs.

Human-AI Jam Sessions

Live music performances become dynamic jam sessions with AI:

1. **AI as the Virtual Bandmate:** Musicians perform alongside AI systems that respond in real-time, generating accompaniments, harmonies, and even improvisations. It's a co-creative exchange on the stage.

2. **Musical Assistants:** During rehearsals, AI acts as a helpful assistant, ensuring musicians stay in tune, maintain tempo, and navigate complex compositions.

3. **Interactive Concerts:** AI analyzes audience reactions and adjusts the performance on the fly, transforming concerts into interactive experiences where music evolves in response to the crowd's energy.

AI's Impact on the Music Industry

The music industry embraces AI as a collaborator and innovator:

1. **AI-Generated Music:** AI composes original pieces used in film scores, advertisements, and standalone albums, demonstrating its versatility across genres and styles.

2. **Personalized Recommendations:** Streaming platforms employ AI to recommend music tailored to individual tastes, reshaping how listeners discover and enjoy new artists and genres.

3. **Production Advancements:** AI-powered software and plugins become indispensable tools for music producers, enhancing sound design, mixing, and mastering capabilities.

Pushing the Creative Horizon

Human-AI collaborations in music push the creative horizon, challenging preconceived notions and expanding the possibilities of musical expression. It's a journey where the boundaries between human and machine blur, creating compositions that resonate deeply with audiences and showcase the remarkable potential of AI in the world of music.

As we explore these dynamic collaborations, we'll uncover stories of composers, performers, and music producers who have harnessed AI as a creative partner. Together, we'll traverse the uncharted territories of this musical landscape, where the music of tomorrow is a symphony of human ingenuity and machine intelligence—a harmonious fusion of tradition, innovation, and limitless creativity.

This section provides an in-depth exploration of the evolving boundaries in human-AI collaborations in music. It highlights the dynamic partnerships between humans and AI algorithms, showcasing how they inspire composers, enhance performances, and transform the music industry. It also emphasizes the limitless creative potential that emerges from these collaborations.

Chapter 4: Personalized Music Recommendations

The Soundtrack of You: AI-Powered Music Curation

Music has an extraordinary power to touch our souls, evoke emotions, and accompany us on life's journey. In an age where our playlists span across genres and eras, the question arises: How do we discover the perfect song for every moment? The answer lies in the world of Personalized Music Recommendations—a where AI becomes our musical curator, crafting playlists that resonate with our unique tastes and emotions.

The Musical Universe

In today's digital age, we are blessed with access to a vast musical universe. Streaming platforms offer libraries with millions of songs, covering every genre imaginable. While this abundance is a treasure trove, it can also be overwhelming. How do we navigate this musical cosmos to find the melodies that truly speak to us?

AI as Your Sonic Guide

This is where AI steps in as your sonic guide. AI algorithms, armed with data on your listening habits, preferences, and even your mood, embark on a mission to curate the perfect soundtrack for your life. They analyze your musical history, your favorite artists, and the context in which you listen to music, creating playlists that are as unique as your fingerprint.

The Future of Sonic Discovery

As we delve deeper into this chapter, we'll explore the evolving landscape of Personalized Music Recommendations. We'll discover how AI is reshaping the way we discover music, the role of algorithms in enhancing our musical horizons, and the impact of personalized playlists on artists and the industry. Join us in this exploration of the sonic future, where music is not just heard but felt, understood, and embraced as a personal soundtrack that accompanies you through life's myriad moments.

Personalized Music Recommendations

In the vast and ever-expanding musical universe, finding the perfect song for a moment, a mood, or a memory can be akin to searching for a needle in a haystack. With millions of songs spanning genres, eras, and emotions, the sheer abundance of musical options is both a treasure and a challenge. How do we navigate this immense soundscape to discover the melodies that truly resonate with us? The answer lies in the world of Personalized Music Recommendations—a space where AI serves as our musical curator, crafting playlists that are as unique as our individual tastes and emotions.

The Soundtrack of Your Life

Music has the extraordinary power to touch our souls, evoke emotions, and accompany us on life's journey. It's the backdrop to our most memorable moments, from celebratory triumphs to quiet contemplations. In today's digital age, our musical preferences have evolved into a rich tapestry, reflecting our diverse personalities and experiences. We are no longer limited to one genre or era; our playlists traverse time and space, mirroring the multifaceted nature of our lives.

AI-Powered Music Curation

The magic behind Personalized Music Recommendations lies in AI-powered algorithms. These digital maestros go to work, sifting through the vast ocean of music data to create sonic experiences tailored exclusively for you. How does this musical magic happen?

1. **Behavioral Analysis:** AI observes your listening behavior with a discerning ear. It notes what you play, when you play it, and how you respond to different tunes. Through this careful observation, it identifies patterns, discovering the genres, moods, and artists that resonate with you on a profound level.

2. **Collaborative Filtering:** Imagine AI as your musical matchmaker. It compares your listening habits with those of other users who share similar tastes. By doing so, it can recommend music that others with akin preferences have enjoyed. It's like having a trusted friend who always knows what song will lift your spirits.

3. **Content Analysis:** AI has an uncanny ability to dissect songs into their individual elements, examining elements like tempo, instrumentation, lyrical themes, and more. Armed with this detailed musical DNA, AI can suggest songs that match your preferences with remarkable precision.

4. **Contextual Understanding:** It's not just about the song; it's about the moment. AI takes into account the context in which you listen to music. Whether you are working out, winding down, or celebrating with friends, it customizes recommendations to suit the occasion.

Balancing Familiarity and Exploration

While AI powers the science of music curation, it's also an art form. It understands that the musical journey is about balance—a delicate dance between the familiar and the unexplored. While it suggests your favorite tracks and artists, it also introduces you to new sounds and genres. It encourages musical exploration, recognizing that the joy of discovery is an integral part of the musical experience.

The Impact on Artists and the Industry

The rise of Personalized Music Recommendations has profound implications for both artists and the music industry as a whole. It creates opportunities for independent and emerging artists to reach new audiences. It challenges the traditional model of radio play and album sales, ushering in an era where listeners have more control over their musical choices. It transforms the music industry into a dynamic ecosystem where the power of AI and human creativity converge.

The Sonic Future

As we delve deeper into this chapter, we'll explore the ever-evolving landscape of Personalized Music Recommendations. We'll discover how AI is reshaping the way we discover, consume, and connect with music. We'll unravel the symbiotic relationship between algorithms and individual expression. Join us on this journey into the sonic future, where music is not just heard but felt, understood, and embraced as a personal soundtrack that accompanies you through life's myriad moments.

This section provides an in-depth exploration of Personalized Music Recommendations, emphasizing how AI algorithms enhance our musical discovery process by tailoring playlists to our individual tastes, moods, and contexts. It also touches on the broader impact of this technology on artists and the music industry, highlighting the dynamic and evolving nature of the musical landscape.

Personalized Music Recommendations: Your Sonic Journey

In the vast expanse of the musical universe, where countless songs weave a tapestry of emotions, moods, and genres, how do you discover that one song that perfectly resonates with your current state of mind? How can you find the melodies that encapsulate your unique musical identity? This is where the enchanting world of Personalized Music Recommendations, powered by AI, comes into play—a world where your musical journey is curated just for you.

The Music of Our Lives

Music is more than just sound; it's a powerful force that shapes our experiences and emotions. It accompanies us on life's rollercoaster, from the highs of celebration to the lows of introspection. In today's digital age, our music libraries have evolved into reflections of our diverse tastes and multifaceted lives. We have the world's musical wealth at our fingertips, but the real challenge lies in navigating this vast ocean of sound to find the gems that resonate with our hearts.

The AI Maestro

Personalized music recommendations are orchestrated by the AI maestro, a digital conductor that wields the magic of algorithms to understand you on a deeply musical level. How does this symphony of personalized music come to life?

1. **Behavioral Analysis:** The AI observes your musical habits with a discerning ear. It pays attention to what you listen to, when you listen to it, and how you respond. This meticulous observation helps it uncover patterns, unveiling the genres, moods, and artists that strike a chord within you.

2. **Collaborative Filtering:** Think of AI as your musical matchmaker. It not only understands your musical preferences but also connects you with others who share similar tastes. This matchmaking process allows AI to recommend songs and artists that align with your unique musical identity.

3. **Content Analysis:** AI possesses the ability to dissect songs into their core elements, examining factors like tempo, instrumentation, lyrical themes, and more. Armed with this detailed musical DNA, it can recommend songs that align with your preferences on a profound level.

4. **Contextual Understanding:** It's not just about the song; it's about the moment. AI considers the context in which you listen to music. Whether you are working, relaxing, exercising, or celebrating, it customizes recommendations to match the occasion, ensuring that the soundtrack of your life is always in harmony with your experiences.

Balancing Familiarity and Exploration

While AI excels at understanding your musical preferences, it also recognizes the importance of musical exploration. It strives to strike a balance between familiarity and the joy of discovery. While it introduces you to your favorite tracks and artists, it also nudges you gently toward new sounds and genres, encouraging your musical horizons to expand.

The Impact on Artists and the Industry

The rise of Personalized Music Recommendations has a profound impact on both artists and the music industry at large. It empowers emerging and independent artists to reach broader audiences, challenging traditional models of music consumption. It transforms the music industry into a dynamic ecosystem where listeners have more control over their musical choices, bridging the gap between artists and their fans.

A Symphony of Personalization

As we journey deeper into this chapter, we'll explore the ever-evolving landscape of Personalized Music Recommendations. We'll delve into how AI is reshaping the way we discover, connect with, and consume music. We'll uncover the art and science behind these recommendations and their transformative influence on the world of music. Join us on this sonic expedition, where the music is not just heard; it's felt, understood, and embraced as a deeply personal soundtrack that accompanies you through the myriad moments of your life.

This section offers an in-depth exploration of Personalized Music Recommendations, highlighting how AI algorithms enhance our musical journey by tailoring playlists to our individual tastes, moods, and contexts. It also touches on the broader impact of this technology on artists and the music industry, emphasizing the dynamic nature of the musical landscape in the digital age.

The Musical Tapestry of Life

Music is more than mere notes; it's the heartbeat of our emotions, the rhythm of our memories, and the backdrop to our daily narratives. It dances with us in moments of celebration, consoles us during times of sorrow, and fuels our creativity when inspiration beckons. In the digital age, our playlists have evolved into intricate tapestries, woven with threads of different genres, artists, and moods. Yet, amidst this rich musical landscape, how do we pinpoint the melodies that truly resonate with our hearts?

Balancing Familiarity and Discovery

AI is not just about playing your favorite tunes on repeat. It recognizes the joy of discovery in the musical journey. While it ensures the comfort of familiarity by recommending songs you love, it also gently nudges you toward new horizons, introducing you to unexplored sounds and genres.

Impact on Artists and the Industry

The rise of Personalized Music Recommendations brings forth a transformative wave that sweeps through both artists and the music industry. It empowers emerging talents to reach a broader audience, challenging traditional models of music distribution and consumption. The music industry itself undergoes a metamorphosis, transitioning into a dynamic ecosystem where listeners have more control over their musical choices.

The AI Conductor

Shaping your musical journey is a task entrusted to the AI conductor— an intricate blend of algorithms and data that listens to your musical heartbeat and orchestrates a symphony of tailored recommendations. How does this enchanting collaboration between humans and machines take shape?

1. **Behavioral Analysis:** The AI conductor pays keen attention to your musical habits, observing what you listen to, when you listen to it, and how you respond. Through this vigilant observation, it discerns patterns that unveil the genres, moods, and artists that resonate most deeply with you.

2. **Collaborative Filtering:** Picture AI as your musical confidante, well-versed in the intricacies of your musical identity. It not only understands your musical inclinations but also connects you with kindred spirits who share similar tastes. This collaborative matchmaking process allows AI to recommend songs and artists that harmonize with your unique musical narrative.

3. **Content Analysis:** AI possesses an innate understanding of the DNA of songs. It dissects them into their core elements—tempo, instrumentation, lyrical themes, and more. With this intimate knowledge of musical intricacies, it crafts recommendations that align perfectly with your preferences, like a tailor creating a bespoke suit.

4. **Contextual Understanding:** Beyond the melody, AI delves into the moment. It considers the context in which you listen to music—be it work, relaxation, exercise, or celebration. It ensures that your musical experience is in tune with the atmosphere, enhancing your connection with the music.

5. **Mood Sensing:** Some AI systems are equipped with mood-sensing capabilities, able to intuitively detect your emotional state and select songs that resonate with your feelings. It offers solace during turbulent times and shares your joys during moments of celebration.

Harmonizing Familiarity and Discovery

Your musical journey with AI is a harmonious balance of familiarity and discovery. While AI ensures the comfort of hearing your favorite tunes, it also recognizes the joy of musical exploration. It gently nudges you toward uncharted sounds and genres, expanding your musical horizons.

Impact on Artists and the Industry

The era of personalized music journeys has a profound impact, not just on listeners, but also on artists and the music industry. Emerging talents gain a platform to reach a wider audience, challenging traditional models of music distribution. The music industry itself undergoes a transformation into a dynamic ecosystem where listeners hold the reins of their musical choices.

The Symphony of Personalization

As we venture deeper into this chapter, we'll explore the ever-evolving field of shaping your musical journey with AI. We'll delve into how AI is revolutionizing the way we discover, connect with, and cherish music. We'll uncover the artistry and science behind these personalized playlists, and we'll witness the transformative influence of this digital conductor on the world of music. Join us on this melodious expedition, where music transcends its auditory form to become a deeply personal guide that accompanies you through the myriad moments of your life.

This section provides a comprehensive exploration of how AI empowers individuals to shape their musical journeys, emphasizing the balance between familiarity and discovery, and highlighting the profound impact of personalized music on artists and the music industry. It invites readers to embark on a melodious expedition guided by AI, where music becomes a deeply personal companion through life's diverse experiences.

Chapter 5: AI-driven Music Marketing

Striking the Right Chord in the Digital Age

In the ever-evolving landscape of the music industry, the journey of a song from creation to the hearts of listeners has undergone a profound transformation. In this digital age, where every note is a click away, how do musicians, labels, and creators ensure that their music reaches its intended audience? The answer is found in the field of AI-driven music marketing—a powerful fusion of art and technology that has become the compass guiding the promotion of music in the modern era.

The Digital Symphony

The digital era has brought both opportunities and challenges for musicians. While it offers unprecedented access to global audiences, it also presents a crowded and noisy marketplace. Standing out amidst the cacophony of digital content requires a strategic approach that combines creativity with data-driven insights. This is where AI steps onto the stage, offering a symphony of solutions to elevate music marketing.

The AI Maestro

AI is not merely a tool; it's the maestro conducting the orchestra of music marketing. It leverages vast datasets and cutting-edge algorithms to make sense of the digital landscape. How does AI orchestrate the art of music marketing?

1. **Audience Insights:** AI delves into the digital footprints of listeners, understanding their preferences, behaviors, and engagement patterns. It

identifies the ideal audience for specific genres and artists, ensuring that music reaches those who resonate with it.

2. **Predictive Analytics:** AI employs predictive analytics to forecast music trends, helping creators and marketers stay ahead of the curve. It identifies emerging genres, styles, and artists that are likely to gain popularity, enabling proactive strategies.

3. **Personalization:** AI crafts personalized marketing campaigns that resonate with individual listeners. It customizes content, messaging, and recommendations to each recipient, fostering a deeper connection between music and audience.

4. **Content Creation:** Some AI systems are capable of generating content, from music reviews to social media posts. This streamlines the content creation process, ensuring a consistent and engaging online presence.

5. **Performance Analysis:** AI meticulously tracks the performance of marketing campaigns, providing real-time insights into what works and what needs adjustment. It optimizes marketing strategies for maximum impact.

6. **Rights Management:** AI aids in copyright and rights management, ensuring that artists and labels receive fair compensation for their work in the digital ecosystem.

The Harmony of Creativity and Data

AI-Driven Music Marketing is not about replacing creativity; it's about enhancing it. It empowers creators, labels, and marketers with data-driven insights that inform creative decisions. It helps craft compelling narratives around music, ensuring that every release becomes a unique and captivating story.

The Impact on the Music Industry

The rise of AI-Driven Music Marketing has had a transformative impact on the music industry. It democratizes promotion, offering emerging artists the tools to compete on a global scale. It reshapes how labels identify and nurture talent, and it creates opportunities for niche genres to thrive.

The Future of Music Promotion

As we venture further into this chapter, we'll explore the dynamic world of AI-Driven Music Marketing. We'll delve into case studies of successful campaigns, showcasing how AI has catapulted artists to stardom. We'll also discuss the ethical considerations of AI in music marketing and the evolving role of human creativity in this digital symphony. Join us on this melodious journey into the future of music promotion, where AI is the conductor guiding music to its rightful audience.

This introduction to Chapter 5 sets the stage for an exploration of AI-Driven Music Marketing, emphasizing the vital role AI plays in helping music reach its intended audience in the digital age. It showcases how AI leverages data-driven insights to enhance creativity and offers real world examples of its impact on the music industry. It invites readers to join the journey into the future of music promotion guided by AI.

AI-Powered Marketing Tools for Musicians: Elevating Your Brand in the Digital Era

In the modern music landscape, the journey from a creative spark to a global audience is no longer just a path walked by the fortunate few. Thanks to the digital revolution, musicians of all backgrounds can share their art with the world. However, with this democratization of music distribution comes a new set of challenges—standing out in a crowded digital arena, reaching the right audience, and making a meaningful connection. This is where AI-powered marketing tools step in as indispensable allies, helping musicians navigate the digital soundscape and amplify their reach.

The Digital Symphony

The digital age has ushered in a musical renaissance. Musicians can now connect with listeners worldwide, breaking geographical barriers and genres. Yet, this vast, interconnected digital world is both a blessing and a challenge. The noise and competition can drown out even the most beautiful melodies. It's in this digital symphony that AI takes center stage, orchestrating a harmonious marketing strategy.

AI as Your Marketing Composer

AI is not merely a tool; it's the composer of your marketing symphony. It wields data-driven insights and algorithmic precision to create marketing strategies that resonate with your audience. How does AI compose this marketing masterpiece?

1. **Audience Segmentation:** AI dissects your audience into micro-segments, understanding their unique tastes, preferences, and behaviors. It ensures that your marketing efforts are tailored to specific listener groups, increasing the resonance of your message.

2. **Predictive Analytics:** AI analyzes vast datasets to predict emerging trends in music and listener preferences. It helps you stay ahead of the curve, creating content and music that aligns with future demands.

3. **Personalized Campaigns:** AI crafts personalized marketing campaigns that speak directly to individual listeners. From tailored emails to social media content, AI ensures that each interaction feels personalized, fostering a stronger bond with your audience.

4. Content Creation Assistance: Some AI tools assist in content creation, generating music reviews, blog posts, and social media updates. This accelerates the content creation process, allowing you to maintain a consistent online presence.

5. Performance Analytics: AI offers real-time analytics on your marketing campaigns, highlighting what is working and where adjustments are needed. It optimizes your strategy for maximum impact.

6. Rights Management: AI aids in rights management, helping musicians and labels protect their intellectual property in the digital space.

The Synergy of Art and Data

AI-powered marketing tools are not about replacing creativity; they're about enhancing it. They provide musicians with valuable data-driven insights that inform creative decisions. They enable artists to tell compelling stories around their music, ensuring that every release becomes a captivating narrative.

The Impact on Musicians

AI-powered marketing tools are a game-changer for musicians:

1. Leveling the Playing Field: Emerging artists can compete on a global scale, reaching audiences that were once out of reach.

2. Niche Opportunities: Musicians in niche genres find their audience with greater ease, allowing their unique sounds to thrive.

3. Efficiency: AI streamlines marketing tasks, saving time and effort that musicians can invest in their craft.

The Future of Music Promotion

As we delve deeper into this section, we'll explore concrete examples of AI-powered marketing tools in action. We'll showcase case studies of successful campaigns and highlight ethical considerations in AI-driven marketing. We'll also discuss the evolving role of human creativity in this digital symphony, where AI is the conductor guiding music to its rightful audience.

This section offers a comprehensive exploration of AI-powered marketing tools for musicians, emphasizing how AI enhances marketing strategies by providing data-driven insights and personalized approaches. It also highlights the transformative impact of these tools on emerging artists and niche genres in the digital music landscape, inviting readers to explore the future of music promotion guided by AI.

Case Studies: Successful AI-Backed Music Marketing Campaigns

In the dynamic world of music marketing, innovation is the key to standing out and reaching a global audience. AI-powered marketing tools have emerged as game-changers, enabling musicians and labels to craft compelling campaigns that resonate with listeners on a personal level. In this section, we'll explore real world case studies of successful AI-backed music marketing campaigns, showcasing how these technologies have revolutionized music promotion.

Case Study 1: Spotify's Discover Weekly

Background: Spotify, one of the world's leading music streaming platforms, launched "Discover Weekly" in 2015. This feature uses AI algorithms to curate personalized playlists for users, introducing them to new music based on their listening habits.

Results: Discover Weekly quickly became a sensation, with millions of users eagerly awaiting their weekly playlist. It significantly increased user engagement and introduced listeners to new artists and genres, benefiting both emerging musicians and established acts.

Key Takeaway: Personalization is the cornerstone of effective music marketing. AI's ability to understand user preferences and deliver tailored recommendations can foster deeper connections between listeners and artists.

Case Study 2: Jukedeck

Background: Jukedeck, an AI-powered music composition platform, allows users to create custom music tracks for various purposes, including advertising and content creation.

Results: Jukedeck's AI-driven approach revolutionized the music creation process. Users, including businesses and content creators, found it cost-effective and efficient to generate high-quality music without the need for a composer. The platform's library grew, covering a wide range of musical styles.

Key Takeaway: AI can democratize music creation, making it accessible to a broader audience and offering businesses a unique tool for branding and marketing.

Case Study 3: IBM Watson Beat

Background: IBM Watson Beat is an AI music composition tool that generates original music based on user input, such as mood and style preferences.

Results: IBM Watson Beat has been used in various creative projects, from video game soundtracks to ad campaigns. Its ability to quickly generate music tailored to specific requirements has made it a valuable asset for creative professionals.

Key Takeaway: AI-powered composition tools can save time and resources in music production, allowing artists and marketers to focus on other aspects of their projects.

Case Study 4: Amper Music

Background: Amper Music is an AI platform that assists musicians in creating original compositions. It offers real-time collaboration, allowing multiple musicians to work together remotely.

Results: Amper Music has empowered musicians to collaborate seamlessly across geographic boundaries. It has also facilitated quick music production for projects with tight deadlines, such as advertisements and short films.

Key Takeaway: AI can enhance collaboration and streamline the music creation process, making it easier for artists to work together and meet project deadlines.

Case Study 5: TikTok's Music Recommendations

Background: TikTok, a popular short-video platform, uses AI algorithms to recommend music tracks to users based on their video content and preferences.

Results: TikTok's music recommendations have helped songs go viral, leading to a surge in popularity for both emerging and established artists. Users often create content around trending tracks, amplifying their reach.

Key Takeaway: AI-driven music recommendations can significantly impact a song's popularity and help artists gain exposure in the digital age.

These case studies demonstrate the transformative power of AI in the music marketing landscape. From personalized playlists to AI-generated music and composition tools, these technologies have opened new avenues for musicians and marketers alike, enabling them to reach wider audiences, streamline production processes, and create more engaging campaigns.

Chapter 6: Challenges and Ethical Considerations

Navigating the Complex Melody of AI in Music

As we have journeyed through the transformative landscape of AI in music production, composition, and marketing, it's essential to pause and acknowledge that this harmonious collaboration between humans and machines is not without its complexities and ethical nuances. In Chapter 6, we delve into the challenges and ethical considerations that arise in the evolving symphony of AI and music.

The Digital Dilemmas

In the digital age, the boundaries between creativity, technology, and ethics blur. AI brings forth a set of unique challenges and ethical questions that demand our attention. From questions about the impact of AI on the livelihood of musicians to concerns about algorithmic bias in music recommendations, this chapter explores the multifaceted facets of the AI-music relationship.

The Challenge of Authenticity

One of the foremost challenges is the preservation of artistic authenticity. When AI systems compose music or generate lyrics, questions arise about the true source of creativity and authorship. We explore whether AI-generated music can ever replace the deeply personal and emotive aspects of human artistry.

The Fair Use of AI

The ethical considerations extend to the fair use of AI-generated music. How do copyright laws and intellectual property rights apply to AI-generated compositions? We delve into the legal and ethical implications surrounding ownership of and royalties in AI-created music.

The Human Touch in Music

While AI has undoubtedly enriched music production, we mustn't forget the indispensable human touch. This chapter contemplates the balance between AI and human creativity and the role of human musicians in a world driven by algorithms.

Bias in Music Recommendations

AI's ability to curate personalized playlists also raises concerns about algorithmic bias. We explore how algorithms can inadvertently reinforce stereotypes and limit musical diversity, along with strategies to mitigate these biases.

Data Privacy and Security

As AI systems collect and analyze vast amounts of user data for Personalized Music Recommendations, questions about data privacy and security become paramount. We discuss the ethical handling of user data and measures to protect personal information.

The Quest for Ethical Guidelines

In a rapidly evolving field, establishing ethical guidelines becomes essential. We explore ongoing efforts to create ethical frameworks and standards that ensure the responsible use of AI in music.

Join the Conversation

This chapter invites you to join the conversation surrounding AI in music by addressing these challenges and ethical considerations. It encourages readers to think critically about the impact of AI on the music industry, the role of musicians, and the ethical principles that should guide our use of these technologies.

As we navigate the complex melodic tapestry of AI in music, it's vital to remain mindful of the challenges and ethical dilemmas it presents. Only by addressing these concerns can we ensure that the symphony of AI and music continues to enrich our lives while respecting the values and principles that define our creative endeavors.

This introduction sets the stage for an exploration of the challenges and ethical considerations associated with AI in music. It highlights the complex issues surrounding authenticity, copyright, algorithmic bias, data privacy, and the role of human creativity in the AI-driven music landscape. It invites readers to engage in critical discussion about how to navigate these complexities responsibly.

Copyright and Ownership in AI-Generated Music: Navigating a Digital Dilemma

In an area such as AI-generated music, where algorithms compose melodies and lyrics, comes the million-dollar question of who retains creative rights for these works. There is a digital dilemma: When questions related to copyright and ownership of AI-generated music call for careful thought, very lucid legal frameworks are required.

The Blurring Lines of Authorship

One of the most intriguing challenges in AI-generated music is the notion of authorship. Traditionally, copyright law attributes authorship to human creators, whether they are composers, lyricists, or performers. However, when AI algorithms autonomously generate music, the lines of authorship blur.

From an ethical perspective, attributing authorship to a machine seems incomplete. Still, it raises questions about the role of human programmers who design these algorithms and input data that guide AI's creative process. Should they be considered co-authors or merely facilitators of AI's creativity?

AI as a Tool for Human Creators

Some argue that AI should be regarded as a tool for human creators, akin to a musical instrument or a recording studio. In this view, the human artist retains the primary creative agency, and AI acts as a means to enhance or streamline the creative process. In such cases, the artist would maintain copyright over the final composition.

However, this perspective doesn't account for instances where AI systems operate autonomously, generating music without direct human intervention. In these cases, the question of authorship becomes more complex.

The Challenge of Defining Creativity

Copyright law hinges on the concept of originality and creativity. It often requires that a work be the product of a human mind to qualify for protection. In the context of AI-generated music, defining creativity becomes a challenge.

AI systems, while capable of generating music, lack consciousness, emotions, and personal experiences. They work by processing vast datasets and patterns to produce compositions that mimic human styles and preferences. This raises questions about whether AI-generated music can genuinely be considered creative or merely a result of sophisticated data processing.

Ownership and Royalties

Ownership and royalty distribution in AI-generated music are intricately linked to questions of authorship. In scenarios where AI operates as a tool for human artists, the existing copyright and royalty frameworks may apply straightforwardly. However, when AI generates music independently, determining ownership and fair compensation becomes more nuanced.

Several models have been proposed to address this challenge:

1. **AI as Work-for-Hire:** Treating AI-generated music as work-for-hire, with the organization or individual that owns the AI system being the owner of the composition. This model aligns with current copyright law but may be seen as restrictive.

2. **Co-Authorship:** Recognizing both AI and human creators as co-authors, with shared ownership and royalties. This approach acknowledges the contributions of both parties but raises questions about the extent of AI's creative agency.

3. **Public Domain:** Considering AI-generated music as part of the public domain, making it freely available to all. This approach challenges traditional copyright models and promotes broader access to AI-generated creations.

The Need for Legal Clarity

As AI-generated music continues to evolve, legal frameworks must adapt to address the unique challenges it presents. The music industry, legal experts, and policymakers are actively debating these issues, seeking to strike a balance between protecting artistic innovation and fostering AI development.

In the absence of clear legal guidelines, agreements between AI developers, artists, and platforms often define ownership and royalty distribution. These agreements can vary widely and may set precedents for future legal interpretations.

Conclusion

Copyright and ownership in AI-generated music represent a complex and evolving landscape. As AI's role in music creation expands, it's essential to establish legal clarity and ethical standards that recognize the contributions of both humans and machines. Navigating this digital dilemma will require collaboration between artists, technologists, legal experts, and policymakers to ensure a fair and harmonious future for AI-generated music.

The Ethics of AI Use in Music Production: Striking the Right Chord

As AI continues to transform the landscape of music production, it brings with it a set of ethical considerations that are integral to shaping the future of music. These considerations revolve around ensuring that AI is harnessed in ways that benefit artists, the industry, and listeners while upholding ethical standards and values.

Preserving Artistic Authenticity

One of the foremost ethical considerations in AI-driven music production is the preservation of artistic authenticity. While AI can generate music that mimics human styles and preferences, it lacks the depth of human emotions, experiences, and creativity. Musicians and producers must be transparent about the role of AI in their work, ensuring that listeners understand the extent of AI's involvement.

Artists should maintain creative agency and use AI as a tool to enhance their work, rather than replace the genuine human expression that lies at the heart of music. Striking the right balance between human artistry and technological assistance is key to preserving the integrity of music production.

Fair Compensation for Artists

As AI takes on various roles in music production, questions arise about how musicians and composers should be compensated. When AI generates music or assists in composition, it's essential to ensure that artists are fairly remunerated for their work.

Transparent agreements and licensing models must be established to define how royalties are distributed when AI is involved. This ensures that artists continue to receive fair compensation, even as AI contributes to the creative process.

Responsible Data Handling

AI-powered music production often relies on large datasets to train algorithms and generate compositions. Ethical considerations related to data handling and privacy come to the forefront. It's crucial to respect the rights of individuals whose data may be used in AI training.

Artists and organizations involved in AI-driven music production must adhere to data protection laws and ethical guidelines. This includes obtaining informed consent when collecting and using data, anonymizing sensitive information, and ensuring the security of data storage and transmission.

Algorithmic Bias and Diversity in Music

AI systems used in music production, such as recommendation algorithms, must be carefully designed to avoid reinforcing bias and limiting musical diversity. These algorithms should promote a wide range of genres, artists, and styles, rather than favoring mainstream or popular choices.

Developers and organizations responsible for AI in music production should regularly audit and refine their algorithms to mitigate bias and promote inclusivity. User feedback and diverse input from musicians and listeners can help in this endeavor.

Transparency and Accountability

Transparency in the use of AI is paramount. Musicians, producers, and organizations should be upfront about the role of AI in music production. This transparency fosters trust among artists and listeners, allowing them to make informed choices about the music they create or consume.

Moreover, establishing accountability for AI-generated content is essential. If an AI system creates music that raises ethical or legal concerns, clear mechanisms should be in place to address and rectify these issues.

Ethical Guidelines and Industry Standards

The music industry, in collaboration with artists, technologists, and regulatory bodies, should develop and adhere to ethical guidelines and industry standards for AI in music production. These guidelines should cover aspects such as transparency, data ethics, fair compensation, and diversity promotion.

By setting clear ethical standards, the industry can ensure that AI is used responsibly and in ways that benefit all stakeholders. This proactive approach safeguards the integrity of music and its cultural significance.

The ethical use of AI in music production is an ongoing conversation that demands the active participation of all stakeholders. By preserving artistic authenticity, ensuring fair compensation, handling data responsibly, mitigating bias, promoting transparency, and establishing ethical guidelines, the music industry can harness the power of AI while upholding its core values and principles. In this way, AI and music can continue to evolve in harmony, enriching the creative and cultural tapestry of society.

Balancing Creativity with Automation in Music Production: A Harmonious Approach

The advent of AI and automation in music production has ushered in a new era of possibilities. Musicians, producers, and composers now have access to powerful tools that can enhance efficiency, inspire creativity, and push the boundaries of musical expression. However, as we embrace these technological advances, it's essential to strike a harmonious balance between human creativity and automation.

The Promise of Automation in Music Production

Automation in music production offers a myriad of advantages:

1. **Efficiency:** Automated tools can streamline repetitive tasks, such as mixing and mastering, allowing artists to focus more on the creative aspects of their work.

2. **Inspiration:** AI-powered composition tools can generate musical ideas and melodies, sparking new creative directions and overcoming creative blocks.

3. **Quality Enhancement:** Automation can help in achieving professional-level sound quality and production standards, even for independent artists with limited resources.

4. **Time Savings:** By automating various production processes, musicians can save valuable time, enabling them to work on more music projects.

Preserving Human Artistry

While automation offers numerous benefits, it's vital to ensure that the essence of human artistry remains at the forefront of music creation:

1. **Authentic Expression:** Music is a deeply personal form of expression, rooted in human emotions, experiences, and stories. Automation should enhance, not replace, the authentic voice of the artist.

2. **Emotional Connection:** The emotional connection between musicians and their audience is a fundamental aspect of music. Automation should not dilute the emotional impact but should amplify it.

3. **Creative Vision:** Musicians have a unique creative vision that sets them apart. Automation tools should be tools for realizing that vision, providing inspiration and support rather than dictating the creative direction.

Strategies for Balance

Achieving a harmonious balance between creativity and automation requires thoughtful strategies:

1. **Selective Use of Automation:** Musicians should selectively choose which aspects of their production process to automate. Routine tasks like tuning vocals or adjusting levels can benefit from automation, while songwriting and artistic expression should remain predominantly human-driven.

2. **Collaboration with Technology:** Musicians can embrace technology as creative collaborators rather than replacements. AI and automation

tools can inspire new ideas, help refine compositions, and enhance the sonic palette.

3. **Human Touch in Performance:** In live performances, the human touch is irreplaceable. Musicians should use technology to enhance their live shows, creating immersive experiences while preserving the authenticity of their performance.

4. **Educational Resources:** Musicians should invest in learning how to use automation tools effectively. Understanding the technology empowers artists to make informed creative decisions.

5. **Feedback and Iteration:** Musicians should seek feedback from peers and listeners to ensure that automation serves the artistic vision. Continuous iteration and refinement are essential.

The future of music production lies in a harmonious partnership between human creativity and automation. Musicians who embrace automation as a creative ally, rather than a replacement, will find new avenues for expression and efficiency in their work. By preserving the authenticity, emotional connection, and unique creative vision that define music, artists can navigate this balance successfully, creating music that resonates deeply with audiences while harnessing the power of technology. In this harmonious interplay, the possibilities for musical innovation are boundless.

Chapter 7: The Future Soundscape

Charting the Uncharted Territories of AI-Driven Music

As we journey through the world of AI-driven music production, composition, and marketing, we inevitably arrive at the horizon of the future—a landscape where creativity knows no bounds, where human artistry and technological innovation dance in synchrony, and where music continues to evolve in ways previously unimagined.

A Symphony of Possibilities

The Future Soundscape promises a symphony of possibilities, where the lines between genres blur, where AI becomes an integral part of the creative process, and where music transcends cultural and linguistic barriers. In this chapter, we venture into uncharted territories, exploring the frontiers of AI-driven music and what lies ahead for musicians, listeners, and the industry as a whole.

The Evolution of Musical Genres

One of the most exciting prospects of the future soundscape is the evolution of musical genres. AI-powered tools can blend and reimagine existing styles, giving rise to entirely new sonic landscapes. Genres become fluid, and experimentation becomes the norm. Musicians are free to explore uncharted territories, merging diverse influences to create music that defies categorization.

AI as Collaborative Muse

AI transforms from a tool into a collaborative muse, inspiring artists with novel ideas and pushing creative boundaries. Composers, producers, and performers find themselves in a dynamic partnership with AI, co-creating music that marries human emotions with machine precision. This union between artistry and technology sparks a wave of innovation, leading to compositions that challenge the very definition of music.

Global Harmony Through Music

AI-powered music transcends linguistic and cultural barriers, fostering global harmony. Language is no longer a barrier to musical expression, as AI systems can generate lyrics and melodies in multiple languages. This inclusivity paves the way for cross-cultural collaborations, where artists from different corners of the world come together to create music that resonates universally.

The Digital Concert Hall

Live performances undergo a digital transformation in the future soundscape. Virtual and augmented reality technologies enable immersive concert experiences, allowing audiences to attend performances from the comfort of their homes. Musicians explore new dimensions of live interaction, blending physical and digital elements to create unforgettable shows.

Ethical Considerations and Boundaries

As we embrace the future of AI-driven music, ethical considerations and boundaries become essential guideposts. We must navigate questions of authorship, ownership, transparency, and the responsible use of technology. The future soundscape invites us to define the rules and principles that will shape the evolving relationship between music and AI.

Join the Journey

In the chapters that follow, we'll embark on a voyage into the future soundscape, exploring its transformative potential and the challenges it presents. We'll encounter visionary artists, innovative technologies, and the ever-evolving intersection of creativity and automation. Join us in charting this exhilarating course as we embrace the future soundscape— a world where music knows no bounds and where the symphony of AI and human expression reaches new heights.

This introduction sets the stage for an exploration of the future of AI-driven music, emphasizing the limitless creative possibilities, the evolution of musical genres, the collaborative relationship between AI and artists, the potential for global harmony, the transformation of live performances, and the ethical considerations that will shape this musical landscape. It invites readers to embark on a journey into uncharted territories where the future of music awaits.

Emerging Trends and Technologies: Shaping the Future of AI-Driven Music

The landscape of AI-driven music is in a constant state of evolution, propelled by cutting-edge technologies and innovative trends. Musicians, producers, and music enthusiasts are at the forefront of this dynamic transformation, embracing emerging trends and technologies that promise to redefine the way we create, produce, and experience music.

1. Generative Adversarial Networks (GANs)

Generative Adversarial Networks, or GANs, have emerged as a powerful force in AI-driven music. These neural networks consist of two components, a generator and a discriminator, engaged in a creative "duel." GANs can compose original music, generate realistic instrument sounds, and even mimic the style of renowned musicians. This technology is pushing the boundaries of what is possible in AI-generated compositions.

2. AI-Powered Collaborations

AI is no longer confined to the role of a creative tool; it's becoming a collaborator. Musicians are exploring AI systems that can jam, improvise, and compose alongside them in real time. These AI collaborators contribute fresh ideas, making music creation a dynamic and interactive process.

3. Neurofeedback and Emotion Analysis

Understanding the emotional impact of music is essential for artists and marketers. Emerging technologies are enabling neurofeedback and emotion analysis to gauge how music affects listeners. AI can analyze physiological responses and emotions in real time, helping musicians tailor their compositions for maximum emotional impact.

4. Virtual and Augmented Reality (VR/AR)

VR technologies are transforming the live music experience. Musicians can perform in immersive virtual concert venues, and fans can attend these shows from the comfort of their homes. AR-enhanced live performances allow artists to merge physical and digital elements, creating captivating visual and auditory experiences.

5. Blockchain for Rights Management

Blockchain technology is revolutionizing rights management in the music industry. Smart contracts enable transparent and automated royalty payments, ensuring that artists receive fair compensation for their work. This technology promises to reshape the relationship between musicians, labels, and streaming platforms.

6. AI-Enhanced Instruments

Musical instruments themselves are evolving with AI integration. AI-enhanced instruments can assist musicians in real time, providing automatic accompaniment, sound synthesis, and even suggesting creative variations. These instruments expand the creative possibilities for artists.

7. AI-Powered Music Education

AI-driven music education platforms are making learning music more accessible and personalized. These platforms use AI to adapt lessons to the individual needs and skill levels of learners, offering interactive and engaging experiences.

8. Realistic AI Singers and Vocal Synthesis

AI is making strides in vocal synthesis, creating realistic AI singers. These virtual vocalists can sing in various styles and languages, opening up new avenues for vocal-driven music production and collaboration.

9. AI in Music Therapy

Music therapy is benefiting from AI applications that help therapists tailor music interventions to individual patient needs. AI analyzes patient data and provides personalized music therapy programs, enhancing therapeutic outcomes.

10. AI in Music Discovery and Recommendation

AI-driven music recommendation systems continue to evolve, helping listeners discover new music that aligns with their tastes. These systems leverage advanced algorithms and deep learning to provide highly personalized playlists and recommendations.

The future of AI-driven music is a vibrant tapestry of innovation and creativity. Emerging trends and technologies are reshaping every aspect of music, from composition to production to the live experience. Musicians and music lovers embracing these developments can unlock new artistic expression and audience engagement. Navigating this ever-changing landscape, it is the symphony of human artistry and AI-driven technology that will take music to new heights and open up a symphony of possibilities in the future.

The Potential Impact of AI on the Music Industry: A Harmonious Revolution

AI is orchestrating a revolution in the music industry, transforming how music is created, produced, distributed, and experienced. The potential impact of AI is nothing short of revolutionary, promising to reshape the industry in profound ways.

1. AI-Generated Music

AI has the ability to compose original music autonomously. It can analyze vast datasets of musical compositions, recognize patterns, and create new pieces that mimic various styles and genres. This opens doors for musicians and composers to explore new creative directions and generate a vast catalog of music quickly.

2. Enhanced Music Production

AI tools are enhancing music production processes. Automated mixing and mastering can optimize audio quality, saving time and resources. AI can also assist in sound design, helping producers create unique sonic landscapes.

3. Personalized Music Experiences

AI-driven music recommendation systems are becoming increasingly sophisticated. They analyze user preferences, listening habits, and contextual factors to curate personalized playlists and recommend new music. This enhances the listener's music discovery experience and keeps them engaged with the platform.

4. Revolutionizing Music Education

AI-powered music education platforms offer personalized lessons, adapt to individual skill levels, and provide real-time feedback. This makes music education more accessible and tailored to each learner's needs.

5. Virtual Concerts and Immersive Experiences

VR technologies are enabling virtual concerts and immersive music experiences. Musicians can perform in virtual venues, and fans can attend from anywhere in the world. This expands artists' reach and creates novel live experiences.

6. Enhanced Collaboration

AI is becoming a creative collaborator for musicians. It can assist in generating musical ideas, suggest chord progressions, and even provide lyrics. Musicians can collaborate with AI to explore new horizons in composition.

7. Rights Management and Fair Compensation

Blockchain technology is revolutionizing rights management and royalty payments. Smart contracts ensure transparent and automatic royalty distribution, benefiting both artists and rights holders.

8. Music Therapy and Wellbeing

AI applications are being used in music therapy to tailor interventions to individual patient needs. This has the potential to improve therapeutic outcomes and make music therapy more accessible.

9. AI-Enhanced Instruments

AI-integrated musical instruments provide musicians with innovative tools. These instruments can offer automatic accompaniment, generate unique sounds, and assist in live performances.

10. Global Music Diversity

AI can break down language barriers by generating lyrics and music in multiple languages. This promotes cross-cultural collaborations and opens up global markets for artists.

The potential impact of AI on the music industry is profound and multifaceted. It promises to democratize music creation, enhance production processes, and offer listeners more personalized experiences. Musicians and industry stakeholders who embrace AI as a creative partner are likely to thrive in this transformative era. While challenges and ethical considerations remain, the harmonious fusion of human artistry and AI-driven technology is poised to elevate music to unprecedented heights, enriching the industry and the musical experiences of audiences worldwide.

Predictions and Speculations: The Future of Music and AI

As we stand on the precipice of a new era in music driven by AI, we cannot help but wonder what lies ahead. While the future is inherently uncertain, we can make educated predictions and engage in informed speculation about the unfolding relationship between AI and music.

1. AI as a Co-Creator

One prediction is that AI will continue to evolve as a creative partner, rather than a replacement, for human musicians. Musicians will collaborate with AI systems that generate ideas, melodies, and harmonies, fostering a dynamic synergy between human artistry and technological innovation.

2. AI-Driven Genre Fusion

AI's ability to analyze and synthesize diverse musical styles may lead to the emergence of entirely new genres and subgenres. Musicians and AI will push the boundaries of genre conventions, creating music that defies traditional categorization.

3. AI-Enhanced Live Performances

VR technologies will redefine live performances. Audiences will attend virtual concerts from the comfort of their homes, where AI and technology will create immersive and interactive experiences that blur the lines between physical and digital worlds.

4. AI Music Superstars

AI-generated musicians may achieve fame and recognition, challenging traditional notions of artistic identity and authorship. We may witness

AI-powered "virtual" bands and artists topping charts and performing in sold-out virtual venues.

5. Music for Personal Growth and Wellbeing

AI-powered music therapy will become more prevalent, offering tailored interventions to enhance mental and emotional wellbeing. AI will analyze individual needs and provide therapeutic music experiences that alleviate stress, anxiety, and depression.

6. AI-Driven Music Production for All

The democratization of music production will continue, with AI tools becoming accessible to a broader audience. Aspiring artists and producers will harness AI to create professional-quality music without extensive technical expertise.

7. AI as a Bridge Between Cultures

AI's language translation capabilities will foster cross-cultural musical collaborations. Artists from different linguistic backgrounds will collaborate effortlessly, expanding the cultural diversity of music.

8. AI in Music Criticism and Analysis

AI systems may play a role in music criticism, analyzing compositions and performances to provide nuanced reviews and insights. Critics may collaborate with AI to deepen their understanding of music.

9. AI-Enhanced Instruments for Live Performance

Musicians will incorporate AI-enhanced instruments into their live performances. These instruments will offer real-time creative support, allowing artists to explore new sonic territories during shows.

10. Continued Ethical Discussions

As AI's role in music deepens, ethical discussions will persist. Questions about copyright, authorship, privacy, and algorithmic bias will require ongoing attention and regulatory frameworks.

While these predictions offer exciting glimpses into the future of music and AI, it's important to approach them with both optimism and caution. The harmonious integration of AI into the music industry will depend on responsible and ethical use, thoughtful collaboration, and a commitment to preserving the authenticity and emotional depth that define music's universal appeal. As we embark on this journey, the possibilities for musical innovation are boundless, promising a future where creativity knows no bounds, and the symphony of AI and human expression reaches new heights.

Predictions and Speculations: Envisioning the Future of AI and Music

The intersection of AI and music is a fertile ground for innovation and transformation. While we cannot predict the future with absolute certainty, we can engage in informed speculation about what lies ahead in the dynamic world of AI and music.

1. AI as a Musical Collaborator

One of the most promising predictions is that AI will increasingly become a creative collaborator for musicians. Musicians will partner with AI systems that assist in composition, arrangement, and even live performances. This partnership will lead to a new era of music creation, blending human emotions with AI precision.

2. AI-Driven Music Personalization

Music recommendation systems will become even more refined, offering highly personalized playlists and music experiences. AI will consider not only your musical preferences but also your mood, location, and activities, curating soundtracks tailored to your life in real time.

3. AI-Generated Genre Fusion

AI's capacity to analyze and merge diverse musical styles may lead to the emergence of entirely new genres and hybrid musical forms. Musicians and AI systems will experiment with genre fusion, producing music that transcends traditional boundaries.

4. AI-Powered Music Therapists

AI will play a crucial role in healthcare, offering music therapy tailored to individual needs. Advanced AI algorithms will analyze physiological and emotional responses to music, enabling personalized therapeutic interventions that address mental health and wellbeing.

5. AI-Enhanced Music Education

Music education will become more accessible and engaging with AI-powered learning platforms. These platforms will provide customized lessons, adapt to the skill levels and learning styles of students, and offer real-time feedback and assessment.

6. VR Concerts

VR will revolutionize the concert experience. Fans will attend virtual concerts from anywhere in the world, immersing themselves in interactive, multisensory performances that blend physical and digital elements.

7. AI Music Superstars

AI-generated musicians and virtual bands may rise to stardom, challenging traditional notions of celebrity and artistic identity. These virtual entities may top charts and sell out virtual venues, captivating global audiences.

8. AI-Enhanced Music Production for All

AI-driven music production tools will become more user-friendly and widely accessible. Aspiring artists and producers will utilize AI to create high-quality music, regardless of their technical expertise.

9. AI in Music Journalism

AI systems may assist music journalists and critics by analyzing compositions, performances, and trends. Music analysis powered by AI may contribute to more nuanced and data-driven music journalism.

10. Ongoing Ethical Discussions

As AI's role in music deepens, ethical discussions will persist. Topics such as copyright, authorship, data privacy, and algorithmic bias will continue to be the subject of debate and regulatory scrutiny.

These predictions foreshadow some really very exciting, high-transformative possibilities that lie ahead in the future of AI in music. While we embrace innovation and creativity, developments such as these must be navigated ethically with responsible use of technology and a commitment to preserving the real heart of music's emotional and cultural significance. The future of AI and music will thus be one harmonious journey of exploration and artistic evolution.

Concluding Thoughts: Enabling AI and Music to Coexist harmoniously for a Vibrant Future.

The convergence of AI and music has ushered in an era of boundless creativity, innovation, and transformation. As we conclude this exploration of the profound impact of AI on the music industry, we find ourselves at the intersection of human artistry and technological ingenuity — a place where the symphony of possibilities knows no bounds.

Throughout this journey, we have witnessed the harmonious partnership between AI and music, each enriching the other. AI has emerged as a versatile collaborator, inspiring musicians, producers, and composers with fresh ideas and novel compositions. It has streamlined music production processes, ensuring professional-quality sound for artists of all levels. AI-driven recommendation systems have personalized music discovery, enabling listeners to embark on sonic journeys tailored to their tastes and moods.

We have also delved into the potential for AI to revolutionize live performances through VR experiences, opening up new avenues for artists to connect with audiences worldwide. AI has taken on roles in music education, therapy, and even journalism, enhancing the accessibility and depth of musical experiences.

As we gaze into the future, our predictions and speculations point to a landscape where AI continues to play a central role in music creation, production, and enjoyment. We envision AI as a co-creator, a bridge between cultures, and a catalyst for genre fusion. We anticipate AI-powered music therapists and music education platforms that cater to individual needs. Virtual concerts and AI-generated music superstars may become commonplace, transcending the limitations of physical venues and human identity.

Yet, amidst this exciting future, we must remain vigilant about ethical considerations and responsible use. Questions of copyright, authorship, privacy, and algorithmic bias will demand ongoing attention and thoughtful regulation. The balance between human artistry and technological innovation will be pivotal in preserving the authenticity and emotional depth of music.

In conclusion, the future of AI and music promises a harmonious symphony where creativity knows no bounds, and technology amplifies the beauty and diversity of human expression. It's a future where artists, industry stakeholders, and music enthusiasts join together in a vibrant and dynamic collaboration. As we embark on this journey, let us remember that the heart and soul of music remain with us, and AI serves as a brilliant companion in our ongoing quest to create, share, and celebrate the universal language of melodies, rhythms, and emotions.

With each note and each algorithm, we move closer to a resonant future where music continues to inspire, heal, and unite us all.

Embracing the AI Revolution in Music Production: Orchestrating the Future

The music industry stands at the cusp of a remarkable transformation, where technology and artistry harmonize to create a new symphony of possibilities. At the heart of this revolution is AI, a powerful tool that has become an indispensable collaborator for musicians, producers, and composers.

The Confluence of Art and Technology

In this era, musicians no longer view AI as a threat to their craft, but rather as a creative partner that augments their abilities. AI algorithms analyze vast datasets, learning from the rich tapestry of musical history to generate compositions that astound and inspire. Musicians now have the privilege of collaborating with AI, inviting it into their creative process to explore new methods of musical expression.

Efficiency Meets Inspiration

AI has brought unprecedented efficiency to music production. Routine tasks such as mixing, mastering, and sound design are streamlined, allowing artists to focus on what truly matters—their artistic vision. AI even assists in generating ideas and melodies, breaking through creative blocks and guiding musicians toward uncharted territories of sonic beauty

The Personalized Soundtrack of Life

Music recommendation systems driven by AI have transformed how we experience music. These systems analyze our musical preferences, moods, and contexts to curate personalized playlists and suggest new tracks. The result? A personalized soundtrack to our lives, enhancing our daily experiences

and deepening our emotional connection to music.

The Future of Live Performance

VR technologies have revolutionized live performances. Musicians transport their audiences into immersive digital worlds, blurring the lines between the physical and virtual. Concertgoers can attend shows from anywhere in the world, becoming active participants in breathtaking audiovisual spectacles.

AI for All

AI democratizes music production, placing powerful tools in the hands of aspiring artists and producers. No longer limited by technical barriers, musicians of all backgrounds can create professional-grade music that resonates with global audiences.

Music Therapy for the Soul

AI-driven music therapy has emerged as a powerful force for mental and emotional wellbeing. It customizes therapeutic interventions to individual needs, offering solace, healing, and inspiration to those in need.

A New Language of Collaboration

AI transcends language barriers, facilitating cross-cultural musical collaborations. Artists from diverse backgrounds come together, weaving threads of harmony that span the globe. AI becomes a universal translator, enabling creative connections that enrich our cultural tapestry.

Ethical Considerations and Responsible Innovation

As we embrace this AI revolution, we must remain vigilant about ethics and responsible innovation. Questions of copyright, data privacy, transparency, and bias must be addressed. The delicate balance between human artistry and AI-driven innovation is essential in preserving the soul of music.

The Ongoing Symphony

The AI revolution in music production is not an end but a beginning—a continuous symphony of exploration and evolution. Musicians, industry stakeholders, and enthusiasts must orchestrate this harmonious collaboration between humanity and technology, ensuring that music remains a vibrant, diverse, and universally cherished art form.

As we navigate this dynamic landscape, we find ourselves on the precipice of endless musical possibilities. Together, we compose the future—a future where music transcends boundaries, heals hearts, and unites souls, guided by the ever-present conductor, AI, in a symphony of innovation and human expression.

Your Journey to the Future of Music: Navigating the Harmonious Confluence of AI and Artistry

As you embark on your journey into the future of music, you are uniquely positioned to explore the harmonious confluence of AI and artistic expression. With your diverse background as a biochemistry graduate, author, singer, coach, sales, and marketing manager, you bring a rich tapestry of experiences to this transformative landscape.

Discovering Your Musical Niche

Your path begins with the exploration of your musical niche—one that seamlessly integrates your passion for AI and your talents as a singer, author, and coach. Consider the following avenues:

1. AI-Driven Music Composition

Leverage AI to aid your songwriting process. AI-powered tools can generate melodies and lyrics that align with your creative vision, providing a unique blend of human emotion and machine precision.

2. Music Coaching and AI Integration

As a vocal instructor and coach, incorporate AI-powered tools into your teaching methods. AI can provide personalized vocal exercises, track progress, and offer real-time feedback to your students.

3. AI in Marketing and Music Promotion

Your background in sales and marketing positions makes you well to explore AI-Driven Music Marketing. Harness AI to analyze audience data, optimize ad campaigns, and target the right listeners for your music

4. Authorship and AI-Generated Lyrics

Merge your passion for writing with AI-generated lyrics. Collaborate with AI systems to create songs that convey powerful narratives and emotions.

5. AI-Enhanced Live Performances

Explore the world of augmented reality (AR) and VR in live music performances. Create immersive experiences that captivate your audience and transcend traditional boundaries.

Embracing Ethical Considerations

As you journey into the future, it's crucial to maintain ethical considerations. Ensure that AI is used responsibly, respecting copyright, privacy, and transparency. Your background in biochemistry can inform your understanding of the ethical implications of AI in music.

Continuous Learning and Adaptation

The landscape of AI and music is ever evolving. Dedicate yourself to continuous learning, staying updated on AI advancements, music technology, and industry trends. Collaborate with fellow AI enthusiasts and musicians to exchange ideas and insights.

Inspiring and Guiding Others

Your role as a coach and instructor can extend beyond music to educate and inspire others about the potential of AI in the arts. Empower aspiring artists to embrace AI as a creative ally rather than a threat.

The Future Awaits

In your journey to the future of music, you are a trailblazer—a creative force poised to harness the transformative power of AI in ways that resonate with your unique talents and passions. As you compose the symphony of your musical future, remember that the possibilities are limitless, and the harmony of AI and artistry is a journey worth taking.

Glossary

1. AI

AI refers to the development of computer systems that can perform tasks that typically require human intelligence, such as learning, reasoning, problem-solving, and creative tasks like music composition.

2. Machine Learning (ML)

Machine learning is a subset of AI that focuses on the development of algorithms and statistical models that enable computer systems to learn and improve from experience, without being explicitly programmed.

3. Deep Learning

Deep learning is a subfield of machine learning that uses artificial neural networks, often with multiple layers (deep neural networks), to analyze and process data, making it particularly suited for tasks like music analysis and generation.

4. Neural Networks

Neural networks are computational models inspired by the human brain. They consist of interconnected nodes (neurons) that process information. In deep learning, neural networks are used for tasks like music generation and analysis.

5. GANs

GANs are a type of neural network architecture where two networks, a generator and a discriminator, compete with each other. GANs are commonly used in music generation to create original compositions.

6. Music Generation

Music generation involves using AI algorithms to compose original music, either autonomously or in collaboration with human musicians.

7. Music Analysis

AI can analyze music to extract information about its structure, instrumentation, harmony, tempo, and other attributes. This analysis can inform music production and recommendation systems.

8. Music Recommendation Systems

AI-powered systems that analyze user preferences and listening habits to suggest personalized playlists, songs, and albums.

9. VR

VR is a technology that creates immersive, computer-generated environments that users can interact with. In music production, VR can be used for creating virtual concert experiences.

10. Augmented Reality (AR)

Augmented reality overlays digital content (such as virtual concert visuals) onto the real world, enhancing live music performances and experiences.

11. Music Therapy

AI-driven music therapy involves using technology to provide tailored music interventions to address mental and emotional health needs.

12. Blockchain

Blockchain technology is used in the music industry for transparent and automated royalty payments, copyright management, and the creation of smart contracts.

13. Algorithmic Bias

Algorithmic bias occurs when AI systems produce biased results due to the data they are trained on. In music, this can lead to biases in recommendation systems or genre classifications.

14. Ethical Considerations

Ethical considerations in AI and music production involve issues like copyright, privacy, transparency, and the responsible use of AI in music creation and distribution.

15. Authorship and Ownership

Questions of authorship and ownership arise when AI systems create music. Determining who owns the rights to AI-generated compositions can be complex and requires legal and ethical considerations.

This glossary should help you navigate the terminology and concepts related to AI and music production, allowing you to explore this exciting field with confidence and clarity.

Resources for Further Exploration

Books:

1. **"How to Make It in the New Music Business" by Ari Herstand**

- This book provides insights into how musicians can leverage technology, including AI, to succeed in the modern music industry.

2. **"Machine Learning for Dummies" by John Paul Mueller and Luca Massaroni**

   - An accessible introduction to machine learning, which is at the core of AI technologies used in music production.

3. **"The Creativity Code: Art and Innovation in the Age of AI" by Marcus du Sautoy**

   - Explores the intersection of AI and creativity, including its impact on music composition and art.

Online Courses:

1. **Coursera (Various Courses)**

   - Coursera offers a range of courses on AI, machine learning, and music. Courses like "AI for Everyone" and "AI in Music" can be particularly informative.

2. **edX (Various Courses)**

   - edX also provides courses on AI and music, including "Introduction to Music Technology" and "Artificial Intelligence in Music."

Websites and Blogs:

1. **Medium (AI and Music Section)**

- Medium hosts numerous articles and blog posts about AI and its impact on music production, written by experts in the field.

2. **OpenAI Blog**

   - OpenAI's blog often features articles related to AI advancements, some of which may touch on AI in music.

3. **MusicTech**

   - MusicTech covers the latest developments in music technology, including AI applications in music production.

Conferences and Events:

1. **International Conference on Computational Creativity (ICCC)**

   - This conference focuses on AI and creativity, including music composition. It's a great place to discover cutting-edge research.

2. **SXSW (South by Southwest)**

   - SXSW often features sessions and discussions on the intersection of technology and music, including AI.

AI-Powered Music Software:

1. **Amper Music**

   - Amper Music offers AI-driven music composition tools that can assist musicians in creating original compositions.

2. **AIVA**

- AIVA is an AI composer that can generate sheet music and audio files based on your input.

Online Communities:

1. **Reddit (r/musicandai)**

   - The "Music and AI" subreddit is a community of enthusiasts discussing AI's impact on music production.

2. **AI in Music LinkedIn Group**

   - Join this LinkedIn group to connect with professionals and researchers working in AI and music.

These resources should provide you with a solid foundation for exploring AI in music production, whether you are interested in creating music, understanding the technology, or staying up to date with the latest developments in this exciting field. Happy exploring!

www.ingramcontent.com/pod-product-compliance
Lightning Source LLC
Chambersburg PA
CBHW071302050326
40690CB00011B/2508